A Small Book
of
Grave Humour

Born in Austria, Fritz Spiegl came to England as a child. He attended Magdalen College School and then studied music at the Royal Academy, while simultaneously training as a graphic designer. He spends his time playing the flute in symphony orchestras, conducting and arranging music, writing and designing books, setting questions for quiz, programmes, including *University Challenge*, and writing a joke column for one of the Liverpool daily papers. He also writes the occasional jingle and signature tune for television.

Fritz Spiegl lives in Liverpool and has a passion for collecting and preserving almost anything, from tombstone inscriptions to newspaper misprints, old cars, barrel organs and four-poster beds.

A Small Book of Grave Humour

Comic & Curious Memorial Inscriptions
Collected by
FRITZ SPIEGL

and recreated by
JANE KNIGHTS

A Pan Original
Pan Books London and Sydney
by arrangement with the Scouse Press, Liverpool

In memory of
Marianne and Walter Neurath

First published 1971 by Pan Books Ltd,
Cavaye Place, London SW10 9PG
4th printing 1976
© Fritz Spiegl 1971
ISBN 0 330 02871 5
Printed and bound in Great Britain by
Cox & Wyman Ltd, London, Reading and Fakenham

Foreword

No amount of 'grubbing in churchyardes' (as that lovable antiquary, John Aubrey, described it) would have made it possible to present all these inscriptions in their original form. For the twin ravages of property development and exposure to our acid-laden atmosphere have taken a great toll of gravestones.

The demand for living-space is constantly rising and it is inevitable that burial grounds have to be sacrificed. In a generation or so, cremation will be the rule rather than the exception.

But all too often, memorials bearing the loving work of ancient craftsmen are now uprooted and used as a cheap source of paving-stones and in no time, messages that were meant to last until the Day of Judgement are worn away by the feet of tourists and worshippers. Unfortunately, many authorities, both church and municipal, appear to be indifferent to the need for preserving their own heritage.

The writers and engravers of English tombstone inscriptions often displayed a deliciously witty turn of phrase in places and situations where one would have expected nothing but solemnity. But our ancestors had to learn to live in close proximity with death: they almost looked upon him as a friend and like any true friend, expected him to take banter in good part.

In consulting previous anthologies (such as those by Andrews, Beable and Diprose) I made some surprising discoveries – notably that anthologists have been merrily anthologizing from each other for nearly two centuries. If I did not always have to get my boots muddy, neither did they, albeit for different reasons.

Nor were they always too concerned with accuracy of transcription; and most telling of all, it transpires that many of the most quoted epitaphs have probably never been on gravestones at all. I was able to trace some of these to a book entitled *THE EPITAPH WRITER: Consisting of Upwards of Six Hundred Original Epitaphs, Moral, Admonitory, Humorous and Satirical . . . by John Bowden* (Chester, 1791). It is a kind of pattern book for the guidance of mourners, a service that survives to this day in the offices of some provincial newspapers, where primitive folk poets are still wielding their craft. Here is a recent example from a Northern evening paper (the names having been altered):

> *Evans, W. H.   In memory of our beloved Dad.*
>   My heart is like a cabbage,
>   A cabbage cut in two,
>   The leaves are all that I have left
>   For my heart died with you.
> *Your loving daughter Ena and son Ern.*

Another funeral verse in the same paper read:

>   How sad it is you've left our side,
>   Through we'll meet when Kingdom come,
>   The gates of Heaven open wide,
>   And in walked Dad.

During the years I spent (on and off) collecting the material for this book, I was fortunate enough to receive help from many friends, notably Sir Bernard Miles, who has an uncanny eye for the quaint and the humorous both in print and in real life, and the Liverpool antiquarian, Glyn Hughes; also the graphic designer, Roger Smith and the incumbents and administrators of numerous places of worship. Unfortunately, it was not possible to include all of their offerings. But most of all I am indebted to Jane Knights for recreating the inscriptions.

We wish to acknowledge to the Council for the Care of Churches permission to quote from the 1947 edition of *The Churchyards Handbook*, which was extensively revised in 1962 and is now being again re-written.

The cover design is based on a tombstone specially engraved for this book by George Thomas, Sculptor and Letter Cutter, of Liverpool.

Liverpool, 1971

F.S.

I do love these ancient ruins:
We never tread upon them, but we set
Our foot upon some reverend history:
And, questionless, here in this open court,
Which now lies naked to the injuries
Of stormy weather, some men lie interr'd,
Lov'd the Church so well, and gave largely to't,
They thought it should have canopied their
bones
Till Dooms-day; but all things have their end:
Churches and cities, which have diseases
like men,
Must have like death that we have.

Webster: *The Duchess of Malfi* (1623)

A Small Book
of
Grave Humour

'The object of an epitaph is to identify the resting place of the mortal remains of a dead person. It should therefore record only such information as is reasonably necessary for that purpose . . .'

The Churchyards Handbook

In Memory

OF

Mrs Phoebe Crewe

who died May 28 1817 aged 77yrs
who, during 40 years
as a Midwife in this City
brought into the world
9730 children

Location uncertain

In Memory of

MRS

LYDIA BARNETT

consort of

NOAH RIPLEY ESQ

By whom she had eight
sons and eleven daughters
seventeen of whom lived
to have families. Her
descendants at the time of
her decease were ninety-
seven grandchildren &
one hundred & six great-
grandchildren

She died June 17 1816 aged 91

Many daughters have done vir-
tuously but thou hast excelled

Brightwell Baldwin, Oxfordshire

'... and perhaps some words which may console or instruct whoever reads it.'

The Churchyards Handbook

Here Lyes

Stephen Rumbold

He lived to y̆ Age of 100 & 1
Sanguine & Strong

An hundred to one
You don't Live so Long

Shifnal

August 7th 1714

MARY

the wife of JOSEPH YATES
of LIZARD COMMON within
this parish,

was buried
aged 127 years

She walked to LONDON
just after the Fire in 1666
was hearty & strong at
120 years
and married a 3rd husband
at 92

Llanrhaiadr, Wales

'The name of the deceased person should be in full, without abbreviation or addition . . .'

The Churchyards Handbook

Here
Lyeth ye body
of JOHN

Ap Robert Ap Porth
Ap David Ap Griffith
Ap David Vaughn
Ap Blethyn Ap Griffith
Ap Meredith Ap Jerworth
Ap Llewellyn Ap Jerom
Ap Heilin Ap Cowryd
Ap Cadvan Ap Alawgwa
Ap Cadell the King of Powys
Who Departed this Life
The xx day of March
In the year of our Lord God
1642
And of his age xcv

Amroth, Pembrokeshire.

According to the parish register,, the original inscription read '24 Years' but the resulting space proved tempting for a joker who, it seems, was also an expert stonemason.

HERE LIETH
The body
of
JOHN REES
Who Departed this Life
Octr the 17th 1824
Aged
249 Years

Reader,
Prepare to meet thy God

Lincoln

'It is only too common to find epitaphs over-
loaded . . .'

The Churchyards Handbook

Here lyeth the body
of
MICHAEL HONEYWOOD DD
Who was grandchild and one
of the threehundred and sixty~
seven persons that MARY the
wife of ROBERT HONYWOOD esq
did see before she died, lawfully
descended from her, viz. sixteen
of her own body 114 grandchildren
288 of the third generation and 9
of the fourth. mrs HONEYWOOD
died in the year 1605 in the
78th year of her age

Unverified. Smokers have always been the subject of moral homilies in verse. There is even a religious song by J. S. Bach entitled 'Elevating Thoughts of a Tobacco Smoker'.

'... with the dead man's activities ...'

The Churchyards Handbook

John Jones Smith of Smoketown

He smoked his cigarette till
from it came
That subtle venom spreading
from its flame
Which poisoned every fibre
of his frame
And laid him low
Yet whilst he smoked he
languishingly sighed
It is but paper round tobacco plied
When like a flicker of a lamp
he died
And rests below

Pewsey, Wiltshire

'... or even those of his relatives.'

The Churchyards Handbook

Here lies the body of

LADY O'LOONEY

Great niece of BURKE

Commonly called the Sublime

She was Bland, Passionate

and deeply Religious, also

she painted in water colours

and sent several pictures

to the Exhibition

She was first Cousin to

LADY JONES

and of such is the

Kingdom of Heaven

St Martin's, Stamford, Lincs

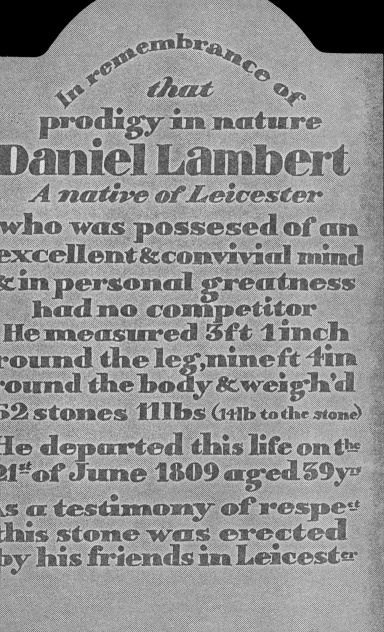

In remembrance of
that
prodigy in nature
Daniel Lambert
A native of Leicester
who was possesed of an
excellent & convivial mind
& in personal greatness
had no competitor
He measured 3ft 1inch
round the leg, nine ft 4in
round the body & weigh'd
52 stones 11 lbs (14lb to the stone)

He departed this life on the
21st of June 1809 aged 39yrs

As a testimony of respect
this stone was erected
by his friends in Leicester

William Bradley, of **Market Weighton,** was known as 'The Yorkshire Giant'.

In memory of

WILLIAM BRADLEY
(of Market Weighton)

who died May 30th 1820
Aged 33 years

He measured
Seven feet nine inches in height
And weighed
Twenty-seven stones

M S
To the pio's Memory
of
RALPH QUELCHE and JANE his wife

who slept } together in 1 { bed by ye space
now sleep } { of 40 years
{ grave till Christ
{ shall awaken them

He } fell asleep AD { 1629 } being { 63 } yeares
She } { 1619 } aged { 59 }

For the } labours { they { ye New lynn built
fruite } { left { twice of yr own
of their } bodies { { chardge
{ one son only
{ and two daughters

Their son being liberally bred
in ye University of Oxon
Thought himself bound to erect
this small monuement
of { their { piety towards { God
{ his { { them

Wigtown, Galloway

Here lies
JOHN TAGGART
of honest fame,
of stature low
&
a leg lame.
Content was he
with portion small
kept a shop in Wigtown
&
that's all

Yorkshire (unverified)

Here
lies

Poor but honeſt
Bryan Tunſtall

He was a moſt expert
angler
Until *Death*, envious of
his mark
Threw out his line,
hooked him
and
Landed him here
the 21ſt day of April
1790

Fort William

SACRED
to

THE MEMORY

of

CAPTAIN

PATRICK

CAMPBELL

who died on the xii of Dec^{em}_{ber}
MDCCCXVI
Aged eighty-three years

A True Highlander
A Sincere Friend
& the best deerstalker
Of his day

Stepney, London

Whoever treadeth on this stone
I pray you tread most neatly
For underneath this same do lie
Your honest friend——
WILL WHEATLY

Ob. November 10 1683

Sudbury, Suffolk

Travellers
I will relate a prodigy

On the day whereon the
aforesaid THOMA͞S CARTER
breathed out his soul
a Sudbury camel passed
through the eye of a nee^dle
GO— and if thou art wealthy
do likewise

farewell

'All statements should be simple, eg, "died" rather than "at rest", or "fallen asleep".'

The Churchyards Handbook

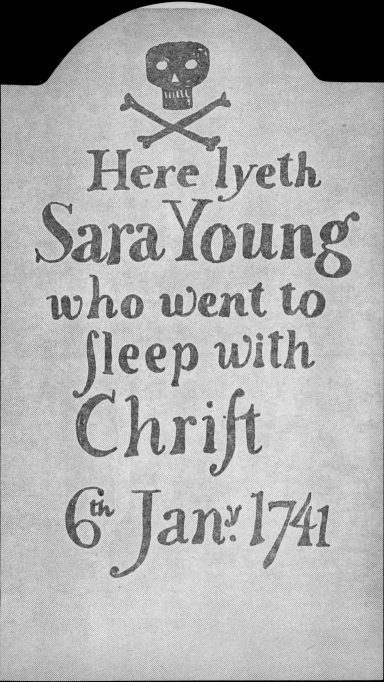

Kendal, Westmorland

UNDERNEATH *this* HUMBLE STONE SLEEPS A SKULL OF NAME UNKNOWN DEEP IN EDEN'S BED TWAS FOUND WAS Ye LUCKLESS OWNER DROWND? WHAT MATTER SINCE WE ALL MUST DYE WHETHER DEATH BE WET OR DRY?

Cross Kirk, Shetland

'It is the duty of the incumbent to refuse to sanction the wording of an intended inscription if it is either verbose . . .'

The Churchyards Handbook

M.S.
DONALD·ROBERTSON

BORN 1st of JANUARY 1785
DIED 4th of JUNE 1848
AGED 63 YEARS

He was a peaceable quiet man, and, to all
appearance a sincere Christian
His death was very much regretted ~
which was caused by the stupidity
of LAWRENCE TULLOCH of Clotherton
who sold him *nitre* instead of *Epsom salts* by
which he was killed in the space of
three hours after taking a dose of it

Edinburgh (not traced)

'. . . or objectionable.'

The Churchyards Handbook

HERE LIE I

MARTIN
ELGINBRODDE

Hae mercy o' my soul
Lord God
A I wad do were I
Lord God
And ye were
Martin Elginbrodde

Dunfermline

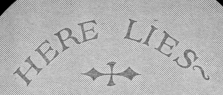

HERE LIES~

JAMES
WILLIAMSON⳨

who died
September 6th 1812

For piety he did excel &
of all the elders
Of his sect, he bore the bell.
Of every web he wove
He stole an ell

Allegedly somewhere in Wales, but unverified.

Here lies
Poor Charlotte
Who died no harlot~
But in her Virginity *
Of the age Nineteen
In this vicinity
Rare to be found
or seen

Edinburgh

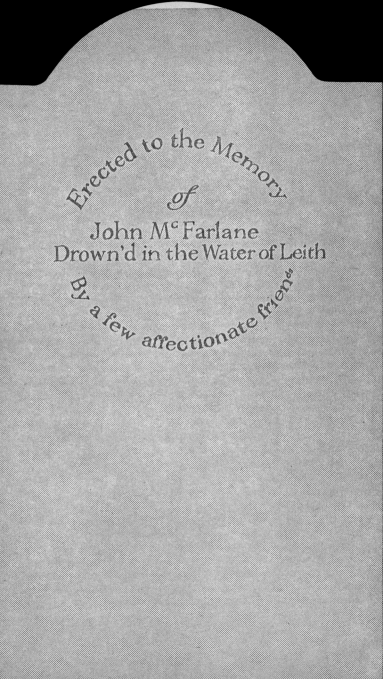

Erected to the Memory
of
John McFarlane
Drown'd in the Water of Leith
By a few affectionate friends

Malta

Here lays

John Tyrwitt

A learned Divine

He died in a Fit
Through drinking Port Wine

April 3rd 1828 Aged 59 years

Pentewan, Cornwall

In this here grave ye see before ye
Lyes berried up a desmal story

A Young Maiden

she was crossed in love
And tooken to the Realms Above

But he that crossed her
I should say
Desarves to go t'other way

Bury St Edmunds

Here lies
interred
the Body of
MARY HASELTON
A young maiden of this town
Born of Roman Catholic parents
And virtuŏsly brought-up
Who being in
The act of prayer
repeating
Her vespers
Was instantaneously
Killed by a
Flash of lightening
August 16 1785
Aged 9 years

Bilston, Staffordshire

In Memory

of

MARY MARIA

wife of Wm Dodd

who died Decr 12th

AD 1847 aged 27

also

of their children LOUISA

who died Decr 12th 1847

aged 9 months, & ALFRED

who died Jany 3rd AD 1848

aged 2 years & 9 months

All victims to the neglect

of sanitary regulation

& specially referred to

in a recent lecture on

Health in this town

And the Lord said to the angel

that destroyed

It is enough

stay now thy hand — 1 Chron.

xx 17

Sutton Coldfield. The murder was the cause of a celebrated law case.

As a WARNING
to *Female Virtue*
And a Humble Monument
of *Female Chastity*
This Stone marks the Grave of

MARY ASHFORD

Who, in the 20th year of her age
Having incautiously repaired to a
Scene of Amusement was
Brutally *Violated* and *Murder'd*
On the 27th of May
1817

Edmonton, Middlesex

'It is nearly always a mistake to mix two or more languages in an inscription.'

The Churchyards Handbook

WILLIAM
NEWBERRY
Who was hostler
to an Inn
& died in 1695 in
confeqence
of having taken
Improper medicine
given him by
a fellow servant

Hic jacet Newberry Will
Vitam finivit cum Cochioe Pill
Quis adminiftravit? Belamy Sue
Quantum Quantita? nefmo—scifue tu?
Ne sutor ulta erepidam

Unverified: The humour lies in the pun contained in the last line and has entered folklore with the limerick

> There was an old fellow from Hyde
> Who fell down a closet and died.
> He had a young brother
> Who fell down another
> And now they're interred side by side.

Here Lyeth ÿ body of

Martn Hyde

He fell down a Midden
and grievously Dy'd

James Hyde

his Brother
fell down another

They now lie interr'd
side by side

St John's Churchyard, Chester

Under this Stone

(lieth)

The Broken Remains

of

STEPHEN JONES

Who had his leg cut off wi'out
the Consent of Wife or Frien^{ds}
on the 23rd October 1842
In which day he died
Aged 31 years

Reader I bid you farewell
May the Lord have mercy on
you in the day of trouble

Banbury, Oxfordshire

To the Memory of
Ric:
Richards

Who by gangrene loſt firſt
a Toe afterwards a Leg
& laſtly his life
On the 7th day of Aprill 1656

A cruell Death to make 3
meals of one
To taſte and taſte till
all was gone
But know thou Tyrant
When the trvmpe ſhall call
He'll find his feet
& ſtand when thou ſhalt fall

Cheltenham

Here Lies
the body of

MOLLY DICKIE
the wife of
HALL DICKIE TAYLOR

Two great fisicians first
My loving husband tried
to cure my pain
in vain
At last he got a third
and
then I died

John Baskerville, the celebrated Birmingham typefounder and printer (1706–75), was a confirmed and determined atheist. He spurned the conventional cross or tablet for his tomb and chose instead a cone-shaped monument with this spirited inscription. However, according to Andrews, it was soon '... overturned and the remains of the man himself desecrated and dispersed until the final day of resurrection, when the atheism which he professed will receive assuredly so complete and overwhelming a refutation.'

Stranger

Beneath this cone in
UNCONSECRATED
Ground
A friend to the liberties
Of mankind
Directed his body
To be inurned

May the example contribute
To emancipate thy mind
From the idle fears of
SUPERSTITION
And the wicked arts
Of priesthood

'There are workmen with thee in abundance, hewers and workers of stone and timber, and all manner of cunning men for every manner of work.'

I Chronicles: **23. 15**

In Memory of

Benjamin Linton
blacksmith

Who died Oct 10 1842 aged 80

His sledge and hammer
lie reclin'd
His bellows too have
lost their wind
Hı His fire's extinct
his forge decayed
His vice all in the dust is
laid
His coal is spent
his iron gone
His last nail's driven
his work is done

IN MEMORY OF

WILLIAM RICHARD PHELPS

(Late Boatswain of H.M.S. Invinsible)

HE ACCOMPANIED LORD ANSON IN HIS
CRUISE ROUND THE WORLD
AND DIED ARRIL 21ST 1789AD

When I was like you
For years not a few,
On the ocean I toil'd
On the line I have broil'd
In Greenland I've shiver'd
Now from hardships deliver'd
Capsized by old Dea[th]
I surrender'd my breath
And now I lie snug
As a bug in a rug

St James's Churchyard, Liverpool. 'The Africa Trade' was a euphemism for the slave trade.

Under this Stone lieth
the body
of
Capt. THOS HUGHES
who departed this life
2nd June 1777
in the 45th year of his age

He was many years a Commander
in the Africa Trade
Which office he filled with the
Great^{est} Industry & Integrity
An Affectionate Husband
And a Tender Father
An Honest Man

His soul serene he meets an angry rod
And cheerfully obeyed the summons of
his God

Therapia, near Constantinople (unverified)

Here rest the remains
of
JOHN COLLINS
A Serjeant of the
Royal Marines
He was one of Englan^{ds}
Gallant Sons
Before Sebastopol was
blown to smithereens
By a charge from the
Russian guns
October 17 1854

. **Woolwich Churchyard** (unverified)

'Publicly to apply one of our Lord's Beatitudes to a member of one's own family must be an error of taste. Similarly, "Well done, thou good and faithful servant"... involves an assumption to ourselves of the right to give verdicts which can be given only by God.'

The Churchyards Handbook

SACRED

to the memory of

MAJOR JAM^es BRUSH

**who was killed by the
accidental discharge of
a pistol by his orderly**

14th APRIL 1831

*well done
good and faithful servant*

Reader take notice

That on ye 12 Feby 176o

Tho. Corbishley

A brave veteran Dragoon

Here went into his
quarters

But remember that when
the trumpet calls

He'll out and march
again

A tombstone in a place called Tombstone, Arizona. Lester Moore was a Wells Fargo agent who was shot in an argument over a consignment.

HERE LIES

LESTER MOORE
FOUR SLUGS
FROM A 44
NO LES
NO MORE

This somewhat dubiously-worded memorial is to the famous Mormon leader who practised polygamy.

BRIGHAM YOUNG

BORN

ON THIS SPOT

1801

A MAN OF MUCH

COURAGE

AND SUPERB

EQUIPMENT

Godalming, Surrey

'An Epitaph should be neither obtrusive nor presumptuous and, in particular, it must not be laudatory.'

The Churchyards Handbook

Sacred

TO THE MEMORY OF~

Nathaniel
Godbold Esq

Inventor & Proprietor
of that Excellent medicine

THE VEGETABLE BALSAM

for the cure of Consumption & Asthmas

He departed this life
the 17th day of Dec'ber 1799

AGED 69 YEARS

Hic cineres ubique Fama

Berkeley, Gloucestershire

Here Lies
the Earl of Suffolk's fool
Men called him Dicky
Pearce
His folly serv'd to
make men laugh
When wit and mirth
were scarce
Poor Dick alas
is dead and gone
What signifies to cry
Dickys enough are still be-
hind to laugh at by and by
Buried June 18 1728 aged 63

Coggeshall, Essex

TO THE MEMORY OF

THOMAS HANSE

LORD THY GRACE IS FREE
WHY NOT FOR ME?

AND THE LORD ANSWERED & SAID
BECAUSE THY DEBTS
AIN'T PAID

Cheltenham

To the Memory of

JOHN HIGGS

Pig Killer

WHO DIED NOVEMBER 26ᵀᴴ 1825
AGED 55 YEARS

Here lies John Higgs
A famous man for killing Pigs.
For killing Pigs was his delight
Both morning afternoon & night.
Both heats & cold he did endure
Which no Physician could cure

His knife is laid his work is done
I hope to Heaven his Soul is gone

ALSO FOUR SONS OF THE ABOVE
WHO DIED IN THEIR INFANCY

Here lies
JAMES EARL~
the Pugilist
who on the
11th of April 1788
gave in

Bolsover, Derbyshire

Here lies
in a horizontal position
the outside case of

THOMAS HINDE
Clock and Watch maker

Who departed this life wound up
in hope of being taken in hand
by his Maker and being
thoroughly cleaned repaired and
set a-going in the world to come

On the 15th of August 1836
In the 19th year of his life

Richmond

ROBERT LIVES ESQ

a Barrister
so great a lover of peace
that when a contention arose
between LIFE & DEATH
he immediately yielded up
the GHOST
to end the dispute

AUGUST 12th 1819

Ashover, Derbyshire. A well-preserved tablet in the church. The original is oval in shape.

TO THE MEMORY

OF

DAVID WALL

WHOSE SUPERIOR PERFORMANCE

ON THE BASSOON

ENDEARED HIM

TO AN EXTENSIVE MUSICAL

ACQUAINTANCE.

HIS SOCIAL LIFE CLOSED ON

THE 4. OF DECEMBER

1796

IN HIS 57. YEAR

All Hallows, Bread Street, London, until 1876, when this beautiful Wren church was demolished to make way for property development. The tombstone also disappeared. Snow was Handel's First Trumpet player for whom he wrote the 'Last Trumpet' obbligato 'The Trumpet Shall Sound' in *The Messiah*.

VALENTINE
SNOW

Thaw evr'y breaſt
Melt evr'y eye with woe
Here's diſſolution
By the hand of Death!
To dirt, to water turned
The faireſt Snow
O the King's Trumpeter
Has loſt his Breath

St Peter's Churchyard, Liverpool. The church (built in 1700) demolished in 1922 and the churchyard built over – a sacrifice on the altar of commerce by the Church Commissioners of the time. However, thanks to local historians, the inscriptions were photographed before being destroyed.

Here the remains
of
ROBERT
LEVER
lies

Who whilst he liv'd did
Ringing highly prize
Then by what he did love
such was his fate
Amongst the Bells his life
did terminate
Therefore ye Ringers all
take care of him
Mischance by Bells before
your glass is runn

He died Oct 24 1761
in the 45th year of his age

Bakewell, Derbyshire

Erected in Remembrance

OF

PHILIP ROE

who died 12th September 1815
aged 52 years

The vocal powr's here let us m^{ark}
Of Philip our late Parish Clerk
In Church none ever heard a layma^n
With a clearer voice say Amen
Who now with Hallelujahs Sound
Like him can make the Roof reboun^d
The Choir lament his Choral Tones
The Town–so soon her$_e$ lie his Bone^s
Sleep undisturbed within
Thy Peaceful Shrine
Till Angels wake Thee ∽
With such notes as thine

St George's Church, Everton, Liverpool

Here
lye
The earthly Remains of

JOHN BERRIDGE

late VICAR OF EVERTON and
an itinerant servant of

JESUS CHRIST

Who loved his MASTER and his
WORK and after running on His
Errands long years was caught up
to wait on Him in HEAVEN

READER

art thou born again
No Salvation without a New Birth
I was born the first February 1716

Derby

JOE RICHARD RILEY

lyeth here

Who lately was our ministere
To the poor he ever was a friend
And gave them all at his last end
This towne must twenty shillings pay
To them for him each Good Friday
God grant all pastors his good mind
That they may leave good deeds behind
He dyed the XXIst of October 1617

Life's like an Inn
Where travellers stay
Some only breakfast
and away~
Others to dinner stay
and are full fed
The oldest only sup
and go to bed
Long is his bill who
lingers out the day
Who goes the soonest
has the least to pay

King's Stanley

ANN
COLLINS

died 11th Sept 1804 aet. 49

Twas as she tript from cask to cask
In at a bung-hole she quickly fell
Suffocation was her task
She had no time to say farewell

Ripon, Yorkshire

Here—lieth

JOHN
JAMES
COOK
of Newby

Who was a faithful
servant
to his master
and an
upright downright
honest man
1760

Composed by Benjamin Franklin for himself,
but his tomb merely reads *Benjamin & Deborah
Franklin, February 1790.*

The body
of
BENJAMIN FRANKLIN
Printer
(Like the cover of an old book,
its contents torn out
And stript
of its lettering and gilding)
Lies here, food for worms
But the work itself s
shall not be lost
For it will, as he believed
appear once more
In a new
and more elegant edition
Revised and corrected
By
The Author

Churchyard of St Michael's, Coventry. Hulm was for sixty years a compositor on a Coventry newspaper.

Here
lies inter'd
the mortal remains
of

JOHN HULM
Printer

who, like an old, worn-out type
battered by frequent use
reposes in the grave
But not without a hope
that at some future time
he might be cast in the mould of righteousness
And safely locked-up
in the chase of immortality

He was distributed from the board of life
on the 9th day of Sept. 1827
Aged 75

Regretted by his employers
and
respected by his fellow artists

Unverified. The hidden inscription reads: BENEATH THIS STONE REPOSETH CLAUD COSTER TRIPE SELLER OF IMPINGTON AS DOTH HIS CONSORT IANE.

'An epitaph of an Englishman should, in an English churchyard, be in the common language.'

The Churchyards Handbook

BENE

A·TH·TH·I·S·S·T

ONERE·POS·ET

H·CLAUD·COSTER·TRIP

E·SELLERO

F·IMP

IN·GT·ONAS·DO

TH·HI

S·C

ON·SOR

T·I·A·N·E

St Nicholas Cemetery, Newcastle

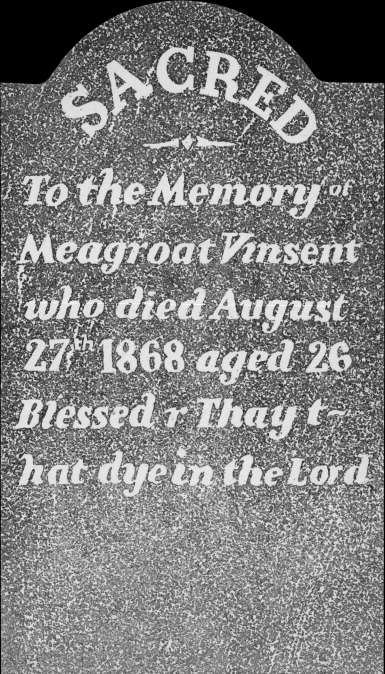

SACRED

To the Memory of
Meagroat Vinsent
who died August
27th 1868 aged 26
Blessed r Thay t~
hat dye in the Lord

'There is an art in writing an epitaph, which, though all think they have it, few really possess.'

The Churchyards Handbook

THORPE'S
CORPSE

Wrexham, Denbighshire

Here lies

I say no more

who was alive
in Sixty-five

Tetbury, Gloucestershire

'... an epitaph becomes public property, and it will be read by those who have no personal interest in the person to whom it refers ...'

The Churchyards Handbook

IN
A VAULT
UNDERNEATH

Lie Interred
Several of the Saunderses
Late of this Parish

PARTICULARS
THE LAST DAY
WILL DISCLOSE

Monkwearmouth

In Memory
of
Sarrah Willcock
Wife of John
Willcock~
Wo died
August 15th 1825
Aged 48 Years

She was But Re Sons For Beds
me To Sa what But think
what a womven should Be
and She was that

Shropshire (unverified)

HERE LYETH

ye body of

MARTHA DIAS

ALWAYS NOISY NOT VERY PIOUS

WHO LIVED TO Ye AGE

of

3sc AND 10

AND GAVE TO WORMS

WHAT SHE REFUS'D

TO MEN

An anagram. Duloe, Cornwall

1629
Marya Arundell

Marya Arundell—Man a dry laurel

Man to the marigold
Compar'd may bee
Men may be liken'd to
the laurell tree
Both feede the eye~
Both pleaſe the optic senſe
Both soone decaeye~
Both ſuddenly fleete hence
What then infer you from
her name but this
Man fades away
Man a dry Laurell is

An anagram (Puckering?). Unverified.

Here lyeth

Mistress
Cissely Pickering

Anagrama
I sleep secure Christ's my King

17 June 1636

An anagram; from St Nicholas' Churchyard,
Great Yarmouth

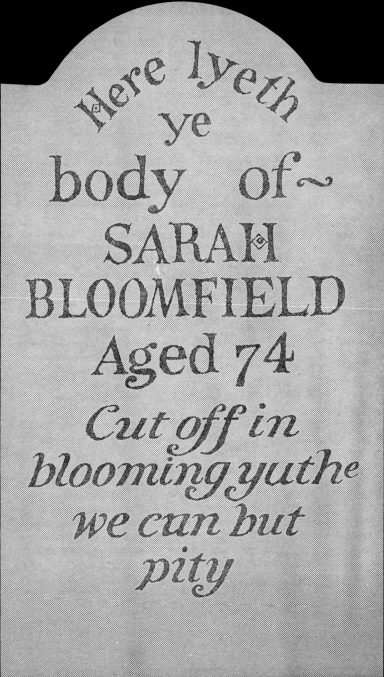

Hastings, Sussex

16 Jan.ʸ 1751

J O S E P H
B A I N

Good peppell as you
pafs by
I pray you on me caft
an I
For as you am fo wounce
wous I
And as i am fo muft
you be
Therefor prepare to
follow me

Dunoon

THO^s WOODCOCK

Here lie the remains of
THOMAS WOODH^{EN}
The most aimiable of
Husbands
And excellent of men

*His real name was Woodcock
But it wouldnt come in Rhyme*

Ireland (unverified)

Here lies

JOHN HIGLEY

whose

FATHER & MOTHER

were drowned

in the Paſſage from America

Had they both lived
they would have been
buried here

Nettlebed, Oxfordshire

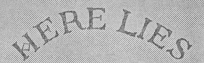

HERE LIES

Father & Mother
And Sister and I
Wee all died within the
space of one short
Year
They all be buried
at Wimble
except I
And I be buried here

Hornsey Cemetery, London

To the memory of

Emma & Maria

LITTLEBOY

the twin children
of
George and Emma
Littleboy of Hornsey~

who died

JULY 16th 1837

two littleboys lie here
yet strange to say
these *little boys* are girls

Alverstone (unverified)

'Till Death us do part . . .'

Book of Common Prayer

Here lies my Wife
Here lies She

Hallelujah
Hallelujee

Potterne, Wiltshire

HERE LIETH

MARY~
the wife of JOHN FORD

WE HOPE HER SOUL IS
GONE TO THE LORD
BUT IF FOR HELL SHE
HAS CHANGED THIS LIFE
SHE HAD BETTER BE THERE
THAN BE
JOHN FORD'S WIFE

1790
MARY FORD

Tiverton, Devon

EDWARD COVRTENAY

Earl of Devon

Hoe Hoe who lyes here
Ye goode Erle of Devonsh^{ire}
With MAUD my Wyff
To mee ful deere
We lyved togeather fyfty ^{yeare}
What wee gave wee have
What wee spent wee hadde
What wee left that wee lost

Streatham, London

Here lies the body of~

ELIZABETH

Wife of

MAJOR GENERAL
HAMILTON

who was married forty seven yrs
And never did *one* thing
To disoblige her husband

She died 18th March 1746

Henaton, Devon

HERE SLEEP A NOBLE PAIR
WHO WERE IN LIFE
HE BEST OF HUSBANDS
SHE OF WIVES THE WIFE

May 18
1660

John and Susanna
Bissell

St Philip's, Birmingham

O
Cruel Death

How could you be so
unkind

To take him before
& leave me behind

You should have taken
both of us if either

Which would have been
more pleasing

To the survivor

Lowestoft

In **Memory**
of

CHARLES WARD

who died May 1770
aged 63 years

A dutiful Son

A loving Brother

and

An affectionate Husb^and

NB *This stone was not erected by*
Susan *his Wife. She erected a stone*
to John Salter *her second husband*
forgeting the affection of Charles
Ward, *her first Husband*

HERE LIES a Lewd Fellow
Who while he drew Breath
I the midſt of Life
Was in Queſt of Death.
Which he quickly obtained
For it coſt him his Life
For being in Bed
With another Man's Wife

Chelmsford, Essex

Martha
Blewit⚜
of the
Swan, Baythorn End
of this Parish
Buried May 7th 1681
Was the wife of 9 Husbands
successively
but the 9th outlived her

*the text to her Funerall
Sermon was
"Last of all the Woman
dyed alsoe"""*

Bury St Edmunds

'According to their just deserts I will judge them.'

Ezekiel 7. 27

SARAH
LLOYD

On the 23rd April 1800
In the 22nd year of her age
Suffered a juſt and ig-
nominious death
For admitting her
Abandoned seducer
In the dwelling-houſe of her
Miſtreſs on the
3rd of October 1799
& becoming the inſtruement
in his hands of the crime of
Robbery & Houſebreaking
These were her laſt words
May my example be a warning to thouſands~

Knaresdale, Northumberland

In Memory
O F
R O B E R T   B A X T E R
of Farhouse
Who died October 4th 1796
Aged 56 years

All you that please these lines
to read
It will cause a tender heart to bleed
I murdered was upon the fell
And by the man I knew full well
By bread and butter
which he'd laid—
I being harmless was betray'd
I hope he will rewarded be
That laid the poison
there for me

Alnwick, Northumberland

Here lieth

MARTIN
ELPHINSTONE

who with his sword
did cut in sunder
the daughter of

SIR HARRY CRISPE

who did his daughter
marry

She was fat and fulsome
But men will sometimes
Eat bacon with their bean
And love the FAT
As well as *lean*

Other Pan books that may interest you
are listed on the following pages

Denys Parsons
Funny Ho Ho and Funny Fantastic 40p

A superb collection of howlers and misprints. 'Cultured
ex-lithographer, white, 45, with gold teeth, desires to get
in touch with seven or eight musically inclined ladies in
search of adventure' CUPID'S COLUMNS, ST PAUL

Funny Convulsing and Funny Confusing 40p

A rollicking new collection of boners and bungles, gaffes and
giggles.

'Milkman, when you leave the milk will you please put coal
on the fire, let the dog out, and put newspapers inside the
door.
PS don't leave any milk' NOTE TO MILKMAN

Funny Ha Ha and Funny Peculiar 40p

For your further enjoyment another collection of clangers
and items of rare fascination – all taken from newspapers
and other published sources. 'A tight hat can be stretched.
First damp the head with steam from a boiling kettle . . .'
SCOTS PAPER

James Herriot
If Only They Could Talk 60p

The genial misadventures of James Herriot, a young vet in the lovely Yorkshire Dales, are enough to make a cat laugh – let alone the animals, if only they could talk.

It Shouldn't Happen to a Vet 60p

'Imagine a *Dr Finlay's Casebook* scripted by Richard Gordon and Thurlow Craig and starring Ronnie Corbett and you will understand why James Herriot is on to a winner . . . a delightful new collection of stories' SUNDAY EXPRESS

Let Sleeping Vets Lie 60p

The hilarious revelations of James Herriot, the now famous vet in the Yorkshire Dales, continue his happy story of everyday trials and tribulations with unwilling animal patients and their richly diverse owners.

James Herriot
Vet in Harness 60p

With the fourth of this superb series James Herriot again takes us on his varied and often hair-raising journeys to still more joyous adventures in the Yorkshire Dales.

'Animal magic . . . James Herriot provokes either a chuckle or a lump in your throat in every chapter' DAILY MIRROR

'Readers of his earlier books are ready to devour their sequel in one gulp . . . he delights in the day-to-day process of living even when things aren't going too well'
NEW YORK TIMES

'His latest success is as full as ever of human and animal oddities' SUNDAY EXPRESS